BOOK ANALYSIS

Written by Alexandre Randal
Translated by Ciaran T.

Mockingbird

BY HARPER LEE

Bright
≡Summaries.com

NELLE HARPER LEE   1

American novelist

TO KILL A MOCKINGBIRD   2

A child's view of the seriousness of the world

SUMMARY   3

CHARACTER STUDY   8

Scout (Jean Louise Finch)
Jem (Jeremy Finch)
Dill (Charles Baker Harris)
Atticus Finch
Calpurnia
Aunt Alexandra
The neighbourhood

ANALYSIS   13

Racial segregation in the United States
Writing through the eyes of a child
A coming-of-age story: from blissful childhood to disillusionment

FURTHER REFLECTION   21

Some questions to think about...

FURTHER READING   24

NELLE HARPER LEE

AMERICAN NOVELIST

- **Born in Alabama in 1926.**
- **Died in 2016.**
- **Notable works:**
  - *To Kill a Mockingbird* (1960), novel
  - *Go Set a Watchman* (2015), novel

Nelle Harper Lee was born in Alabama in 1926. She began studying for a law degree before leaving to live in New York, where she found a job in an airline company. However, this was just to make ends meet – Lee spent all of her free time writing. *To Kill a Mockingbird* was published in 1960 and quickly became an international success. It was adapted for the cinema two years later by Robert Mulligan, with Gregory Peck in the role of Atticus Finch.

To Kill a Mockingbird was the only book Lee published for a long time, and even today her life remains a mystery. However, in 2015, a second book by Lee, Go Set a Watchman, was published, to the great surprise of the literary world. She died in February 2016.

TO KILL A MOCKINGBIRD

A CHILD'S VIEW OF THE SERIOUSNESS OF THE WORLD

- **Genre**: novel
- **Reference edition**: Lee, H. (1962) *To Kill a Mockingbird*. New York: Popular Library.
- **1st edition**: 1960
- **Themes**: childhood, racism, disillusionment, intolerance, trial

To Kill a Mockingbird was published in 1960 in North America, right in the midst of the Civil Rights Movement, and won the Pulitzer Prize in 1961. It has sold more than 30 million copies worldwide and has been translated into 40 languages. Lee's coming-of-age story describes a few months in the life of Scout, a 7-year-old girl, as her father, a lawyer, defends a black man accused of raping a white woman.

The story takes place in a little town in Alabama during the 1930s at the time of the Great Depression. Although the plot focuses on the serious matters of racism and everyday stupidity, childhood memories bring a certain degree of light-heartedness to the novel, and the story is brightened by Scout's naïve, and often amusing, view of the world.

SUMMARY

The novel is set in 1930s Maycomb, Alabama. Scout and Jem Finch, aged six and ten years old respectively, live near a house which both intrigues and terrifies them. It belongs to the Radleys, a strange family who live in reclusion. During the holidays, they meet a boy called Dill who is staying with his aunt. The three children very quickly become friends. They start to play together and, the following summer, invent a game about the Radleys, in spite of being forbidden to do so by Atticus, Scout and Jem's father. One night, the children venture onto the Radleys' veranda. A shadow suddenly appears, startling them. A gunshot rings out and they scamper, terrified. In his panic, Jem manages to lose his trousers. When they get home, Dill makes up a plausible, if rather stupid, excuse as an explanation.

In September, Scout starts school, but she is disappointed in her teacher, Miss Caroline, as her teaching methods do not fit the poor children of Maycomb. Scout, who learnt how to read and write long before she started school, incurs the wrath of the teacher and is forbidden from reading, a terrible punishment for a girl who adores deciphering the newspaper with her father. After such a disappointing day, the little girl loses all desire to go to school. Her father therefore suggests a compromise: he will let her continue to read the newspaper with him if she agrees to go back to school. She accepts. One day, while on her way home, she finds some chewing gum hidden in a tree in front of the Radleys' house. This happens again several times. However, one morning, Jem is upset to discover that the opening has been blocked up with cement.

Winter comes and brings snow along with it, which is a very unusual event for Maycomb. There is no school that day, and Jem and Scout makes their first ever snowman. During the night, Atticus wakes the children up and makes them go outside, because the house next door is on fire. Without Scout noticing, Arthur Radley covers her shoulders with a blanket.

Since the father of the two children is a lawyer, he is appointed by the court to defend Tom Robinson, a black man accused of raping a white woman. Criticism of Atticus begins to get violent at school and in town, and Scout fights another pupil who teases her about the case. Her father tries to prepare her for the trial which is coming up and the consequences it will have for their family. One day, while on their way to town, Scout and Jem pass the house of Mrs Dubose, a sick, old, bad-tempered woman who provokes them about the trial. Jem is furious and ruins her flowers. Atticus orders him to go and apologise. Mrs Dubose demands that he read to her for a month in compensation. As a result, the two children go to the old woman's house every day. After she dies, they find out that their presence helped her to detox from morphine.

With Tom Robinson's trial approaching, hostile reactions against Scout's family continue to increase. One night, feeling that things are about to go sour, Atticus goes to the prison to watch over the defendant. The children, intrigued to see him go out so late, follow him. They witness a heated argument between their father and some farmers who have come to lynch the prisoner. Even if she does not totally understand what is going on, Scout's naïveté manages to diffuse the situation. At Christmas, Uncle Jack comes to visit them, and then they go to see Aunt Alexandra, a narrow-minded woman who is quick to criticise. She has a grandson the same age as Scout, and the two children argue about the trial.

Jem begins to change: he gets bigger and starts spending more time on his own, and Scout begins to understand him less and less. She finds out that Dill will not be coming this summer. However, one night, the two children find the little boy hidden under a bed, and it turns out that he has run away from home to be with them. Atticus agrees to let him stay for a couple of days. Aunt Alexandra also comes to live with them. However, living with her is difficult and a lot of arguments break out.

On the day of the trial, the whole region seems to have come to court. The children go too and, since there are no seats left, they are allowed to sit in the area reserved for black people. The trial begins with the testimony of Bob Ewell, the father of the young woman who claims to have been raped. The Ewells are among the poorest and most looked-down-upon residents of the town. Atticus casts doubt on the fact that the defendant, who has a maimed arm, managed to injure Mayella, the alleged victim.

When the girl is questioned, her testimony is confused and highlights her miserable living conditions. Nevertheless, she continues to accuse Tom Robinson of raping and beating her. Finally, it is the defendant's turn to speak: he describes a lonely girl who invited him home and, after being rebuffed by Tom and caught by her father, made up this rape story. Atticus supports this version of events and points out the racial prejudices at play in the case. Nevertheless, the defendant is declared guilty, which comes as a shock to the children.

The next morning, Atticus is moved to discover that the black community has thanked him by leaving a pile of food on the veranda. He goes back into town, where Bob Ewell spits at him and threatens him. Later on, Atticus comes home after learning that Tom Robinson has been killed while attempting to escape.

Alexandra organises afternoon tea with the ladies of Maycomb. Scout does not feel at all comfortable in this little meeting exclusively for women and does not understand what is going on. However, she is impressed that her aunt is facing the situation with such humanity and courage, and therefore rethinks her opinion on her and on becoming a lady.

When school starts back, Jem, who is growing up, begins to spend even more time on his own. Even though Scout is less terrified by the Radley house now, that does not mean she is any less intrigued by it.

What is more, apart from several incidents with Bob Ewell, things seem to be getting back to normal for Atticus. On Halloween, Scout is supposed to take part in a show about the history of the town in which the children parade around dressed up as items of food – Scout is a ham. However, during the show, she falls asleep backstage and misses her cue. Ashamed, she refuses to take her ham costume off when it is time to go home.

On the way, Jem and Scout are attacked. They are saved by Arthur Radley. When the sheriff arrives at the scene, he finds Bob Ewell stabbed to death. It is clear that he had attempted to kill the children. Atticus believes that Jem is the one who killed him while trying to defend himself. However, the sheriff is quick to correct him, showing him that it was Arthur Radley who stabbed Bob Ewell, but makes it clear that it would be better not to let this get around town.

Scout goes with their saviour to his house. She imagines herself in his shoes, watching her and her brother playing on the street, and reminisces about the events of the past few months.

CHARACTER STUDY

SCOUT (JEAN LOUISE FINCH)

Jean Louise Finch, nicknamed Scout, is the heroine and narrator of the book. She is six years old at the beginning of the story. She is a little girl with a sharp mind, a bit of a tomboy (she does not think twice before punching people who annoy her), and is very attached to Jem, her older brother. The two are very close. She does have friends too, but none of them are girls and, curiously enough, there are no other female characters her age in the book.

She is a child who thinks deeply about things and analyses the people around her: she asks them lots of questions, tries to understand and is always observing those around her. At times innocent, at others exceptionally lucid, she does not always know how to interpret the adult world, which remains a constant source of perplexity for her. Her humorous view of the world highlights the absurdities and contradictions of society's rules, and also illustrates the egocentric, naïve side of childhood.

Impulsive and carefree at the beginning of the novel, she becomes wiser and more mature as the months go by and she is confronted with evil (racism, injustice). Her father leads her to make a compromise between accepting the real world and respecting basic moral principles.

JEM (JEREMY FINCH)

Scout's brother Jem is four years older than she is, and also develops over the course of the story: he goes from being a little boy to a future young man. He plays the role of big brother to perfection, bringing Scout along on the majority of his adventures, and he both protects and comforts his little sister depending on the situation. Most importantly, he is her 'theoretician of life': since he is older, he can explain his perception of the world to his younger sibling.

Unlike Scout, who was too small to remember much, he has sad memories of their mother, as she died several years ago, and he is sometimes overwhelmed with nostalgia.

DILL (CHARLES BAKER HARRIS)

Scout and Jem's friend Dill is an orphan who spends the summer holidays with their neighbour Miss Rachel Haverford, who he calls his aunt. He has a very active imagination and is always inventing unbelievable stories. He says he is engaged to Scout, sending her sweet letters and sometimes stealing kisses from her when her brother is not looking. His character was inspired by the American writer Truman Capote (1924-1984), a friend of Lee's who she knew since she was a child.

ATTICUS FINCH

Atticus is Scout and Jem's father. Around 50 years old, he is a widower who raises his two children alone according to his principles, which are rather liberal for the time. As a lawyer, he takes the defence of Tom Robinson very seriously. However, he knows he is fighting a losing battle, even though it is clear that the black man has been unjustly accused of rape.

Atticus is an understanding father, and also proves to be an astute psychologist, understanding how to balance severity and leniency according to the situation. The freedom he raises Scout and Jem in is not always viewed positively in Maycomb: his sister criticises him for raising them like savages and, worst of all, he lets his daughter parade around in dungarees instead of a pretty dress like all the other girls her age.

Atticus is a crucial point of reference for the narrator throughout the story. Although he demands a lot from his daughter, he also respects her enormously. His love, just like his tender, understanding attitude, helps the little girl to stay on the right path.

He treats his children with respect and speaks to them like adults, but never forgets that they have limits. As a result, he does not lie to them and does not try to hide things from them when they ask him questions. On the contrary, he tries to give them the tools they need to understand the world and prepare them for the future. Even during conflicts and hard times, he teaches his children to put themselves in other people's shoes instead of getting carried away by hate or contempt, and constantly tells them that they should avoid judging people.

While it is true that he teaches them a lot through education and discussion, he also does so by example. He is an honest, profoundly humane man who does not hesitate to defend a lost cause, because someone has to do it and he is strong enough to bear this weight. He is an almost Christlike character, tasked by others with facing what they do not have the courage to stand up to, carrying the weight of an unjust, unequal society. In this sense, the trial is his "Stations of the Cross", with his final failure the announcement of the verdict. However, he is able to overcome his ordeal and put a positive spin on things. He therefore teaches his children a great deal about courage and dignity, which fits the character we see throughout the story.

In any case, he is a very modern father in this little rural town in the Deep South of the United States during the 1930s.

CALPURNIA

Calpurnia, the Finches' black cook, is a part of the family and serves as a sort of adoptive mother to the children, since their real mother died when they were very young. Just like Atticus Finch, she is strict but fair, and agrees with him on the majority of educational and moral principles he instils in his children. One of the few people among the black community who know how to read, she is the one who teaches Scout how to write.

AUNT ALEXANDRA

Aunt Alexandra, Atticus' sister, lives in a world with strict rules and does not approve of the way her brother brings up his children. She thinks it is her place to help raise her niece and nephew and tries to make Scout into a 'proper' young lady, forcing her to wear dresses and go to the afternoon teas she organises with the ladies of Maycomb.

Be that as it may, she is loyal to Atticus and supports him during and after the difficult time of Tom Robinson's trial, at which point she reveals herself to be more humane than she first seemed.

THE NEIGHBOURHOOD

In this little town where everyone knows everyone, neighbourhoods are very tight-knit groups. Scout knows which neighbours are hostile or indifferent to her (like Miss Stephanie Crawford, an inquisitive gossip with a loose tongue who is always ready to bad-mouth others) and those she can count on, like Miss Maudie Atkinson, a widow who is the same age as her father and who shares his broad-mindedness and noble ideas.

One of the neighbouring houses piques the curiosity of the whole town, particularly the Finch children. The house belongs to the Radley family, who nobody ever sees. One of the sons, Arthur, also known as "Boo", is rumoured to have committed heinous crimes.

ANALYSIS

RACIAL SEGREGATION IN THE UNITED STATES

Racism and intolerance in 1930s rural America

Although the novel is centred around racism, through the trial of a black man, segregation and the rules which govern relationships between the white and black communities are also an underlying presence throughout the story. This reflects the reality of the time: the two groups lived separately, and injustice and racism were simply a part of the black community's daily lives. It should be noted that many of the major victories of the Civil Rights Movement were only won in the 1960s, after the novel had already been written.

In this respect, the Finches are the odd ones out in society. Atticus treats all men the same, whether they are white or black, rich or poor, educated or illiterate. Calpurnia appears to be a part of the family, and he sees nothing wrong with letting his daughter visit her in the black part of town, nor with his children going to a black church. This kind of attitude goes directly against the societal norms of that time, and Atticus is therefore sometimes forced to argue with his own family, like when his sister Alexandra suggests that he let his cook go.

The racist attitude of the majority of people in Maycomb County is due to the general intolerance of difference. Adults seem to be caught up in a network of strict rules and principles which dictate their behaviour and govern relations between them. Take Mr Dolphus Raymond, for instance, who married a black woman: he pretends to be a drunk in order to be left in peace, as his alcoholism is a good enough reason for his difference in the eyes of the other residents. Bigotry and sectarianism, which are privileges that only the white community have, are sentiments which are shared by a number of close-minded and often ridiculous characters. Aunt Alexandra is one of these characters, as she is full of unshakeable principles on what should and should not be done, the people who one can associate with, the clothes a lady should wear, and so on. These views can often be seen in the female characters of the novel: aside from Alexandra, Stephanie Crawford is the embodiment of passive racism, while Miss Caroline, Scout's first teacher, turns out to be quite simply out of step with the time and place she lives in, as her thoughts on teaching are completely unsuited for the poor, rural environment where she teaches.

Rurality and urbanity and poverty and wealth are also a part of the value system in this society where everyone has a defined role, particularly during the troubled times of the Great Depression – a time of economic crisis, widespread unemployment and famine following the Wall Street Crash of 1929, the repercussions of which allowed Adolf Hitler (1889-1945) to come to power in Europe. As a result, the barriers between the races are insurmountable, and the few people who attempt to bypass them pay a heavy price, like Mayella Ewell, for example, the young girl who claims to have been raped by Tom Robinson.

GO SET A WATCHMAN

Go Set a Watchman, Lee's second novel, came out in July 2015. Even though the book was written in 1957, and therefore before *To Kill a Mockingbird*, it is presented as the sequel to the first novel. The story takes place 20 years after the events of *To Kill A Mockingbird*, during the 1950s. Scout is now 26 years old and lives in New York. She comes back to visit her hometown of Maycomb, which is the literary equivalent of Monroeville, where Lee was born. However, Scout quickly realises that her father, Atticus Finch, despite being a humanist, the lawyer who defended Tom Robinson and a defender of black emancipation 20 years ago, is no longer the knight in shining armour she remembers from her childhood. Now, he even comes out with racist remarks himself. According to Pierre Demarty, the French translator of the second novel: "She transformed a morally and politically ambiguous novel into a more accessible, universal one. *Watchman* is a much darker book, and presents a much more critical, pessimistic view of society"[1] (Broue, 2015).

The release of the book was met with an unusual amount of hype from the English-speaking media, and the novel shattered sales records just a few weeks after it was published.

---

1. This quotation has been translated by BrightSummaries.com.

Laws to ratify racism

After the American Civil War (1861-1865) and the abolition of slavery in 1865, the whole country found itself in a period of transition known as Reconstruction. It was at this time that official racial segregation began, and lasted from 1876 to 1965. Indeed, from 1876 onwards, various laws were introduced in the Southern States of America to legally differentiate citizens according to their ethnicity. At this point, a *de jure* system of segregation came into force and remained in place in the South for around a century.

Following this legislation, African-Americans were subjected to many discriminatory, racist acts, which sometimes went as far as lynchings and murders. In Alabama, for example, where *To Kill a Mockingbird* takes place, motorway service stations were made to have counters and waiting rooms separated according to skin colour. Howard Zinn (American historian, 1922-2010) highlights the fact that "in the years between 1889 and 1903, on the average, every week, two Negroes were lynched by mobs – hanged, burned, mutilated" (Zinn, 2002: 315). Moreover, a 2015 study estimated that around 4000 African-Americans were lynched during the period from 1877 to 1950. A map of the South of the United States drawn up by *The New York Times* indexes these 73 years of lynchings ("Map of 73 Years of Lynchings", *New York Times*, 2015). These acts, committed by white people, were a common occurrence and often ended with hangings.

What is more, the court often gave unjust rulings, like during the 1931 Scottsboro Case. This trial was an important stage in the fight against racial discrimination, and was no doubt an important factor in the writing of Lee's novel, as she set her story during the same time period. On 25 March 1931 in Scottsboro, Alabama, two young white women falsely accused nine black teenagers, aged between 13 and 19, of raping them. Eight of the young men were sentenced to death by hanging, without any proof of their guilt. The ILD (International Labor Defense), an organisation committed to the defence of civil rights, managed to delay the executions and appeal the ruling. A long political battle then began, lasting for 15 years until 1946, when the last of the men was finally freed. This has become an emblematic episode in the fight for racial equality in the United States and, in many respects, paved the way for the Civil Rights Movement.

DID YOU KNOW?

Lee was not only one to be marked by these events. Jean-Paul Sartre (French writer, 1905-1980) was inspired by this trial to write his play *The Respectful Prostitute* (1946).

On 1 December 1955, Rosa Parks (1913-2005) became the heroine of another symbolic event in the fight for change in both the law and in people's mentalities. One day in Montgomery, Alabama, the 42-year-old seamstress refused to give up her seat on the bus for a white passenger and received a fine. An anti-segregation movement, led by a young pastor called Martin Luther King, then organised a city-wide bus boycott. Segregation in American buses was finally revoked on 13 November 1956. This was the first victory for the Civil Rights Movement and signalled the start of a long battle for the complete abolition of racial segregation.

It was only on 2 July 1964 that racial segregation was completely outlawed throughout the country with the introduction of the Civil Rights Act. On 6 August the following year, black Americans' right to vote was reaffirmed. However, fighting to change mentalities turned out to be a far more time-consuming task, and racial discrimination is still unfortunately far too frequent in the United States. As a result, *To Kill a Mockingbird* quickly became a cult novel of modern American literature, and remains just as popular today.

WRITING THROUGH THE EYES OF A CHILD

To Kill a Mockingbird is a novel about childhood. Narrated by Scout, who is six at the start of the story and nine at the end, the novel presents us with a dual perspective of society, at once naïve and exceptionally lucid, and sometimes even bordering on cynicism. In this respect, the reader can feel the presence of an adult writer using this childish narrator to mix occasionally simplistic analyses with the cruellest of realities. Even when Scout is wrong and misinterprets the situation, the author intervenes with a shift in tone which shows the error of the young narrator. The effect is mostly comical and the novel has a very humorous tone from start to finish.

The binary nature of the narration, with the contrast between the summer holidays and termtime, highlights the extent to which holidays symbolise freedom for children. They are the time for games, discovery, learning and maturing. The days sometimes seem to stretch out for an eternity, while the time spent in school, with the sole exception of Scout's first day, which is described in minute detail, is barely mentioned and could be described as a systematic temporal ellipsis.

A COMING-OF-AGE STORY: FROM BLISSFUL CHILDHOOD TO DISILLUSIONMENT

The two main characters, Scout and her brother Jem, grow up before the reader's eyes and go from being naïve children to the young adults they will become. Their personal development is traced in a series of anecdotes: the book sometimes appears more like a collection of short stories to be read independently from one another than an actual novel. Some are light-hearted, while others deal with more serious matters. Each little story seems to give the children the chance to learn a life lesson, to discover a feature of human nature and, at the same time, to learn how to understand other people and accept their differences. Their father is a guide in the truest sense of the word, a just, far-sighted man who never lets himself be caught up in negative or overly subjective emotions.

The reader witnesses Scout changing more than any other character, given that she is the narrator. As the story progresses, she experiences a string of disappointments. First, she has to give up on her idealistic image of school, because she realises that she will never learn anything there. She also learns to stop relying on her brother as much because, as he is getting older, he sometimes needs to go off on his own and – in doing so – breaks their sibling bond. Nevertheless, by distancing herself from him, she ends up being able to accept the idea of becoming a woman. She sees her aunt as a female role model, having finally discovered that the older woman has some admirable qualities.

The trial shows Scout, Jem and Dill the extent to which human justice is flawed and unjust, a reflection of the adult world which seems harsh and cruel. However, Atticus' view on the matter gives them a glimmer of hope and tolerance. Indeed, the lawyer is able to find the few drops of positivity in a sea of disasters. Faced with the unjust verdict of the jury, he explains to his children that he still got something out of Tom Robinson's trial: the jury did not simply rule automatically in favour of the white person, but actually gave the case due consideration. Progress has clearly been made. In doing so, he also comforts himself, because the outcome of the trial was a hard blow for him, even though he saw it coming.

At the very end of the novel, after the children are attacked by Bob Ewell, Scout realises how much all these events have forced her and her brother to mature: "I thought Jem and I would get grown but there wasn't much else left for us to learn, except possibly algebra."

FURTHER REFLECTION

SOME QUESTIONS TO THINK ABOUT...

- History, whether the kind found in books (the American Civil War) or the individual kind (the Finch family tree) is often touched upon in the novel. How is it related to what Scout goes through?
- Routine and rules govern the lives of the residents of Maycomb. Does this lead to a kind of sterility? Or is this a sort of helpful screen to break free of certain restrictions?
- Look at how the female figures in the novel play an important role in the transmission of rules and highlight their main characteristics. Could it be said that the most positive female characters are the ones who are most like men?
- Black and white people live side by side, but they know little about each other and inhabit two totally different worlds. At which points in the novel do these universes truly collide?
- In what way is the trial similar to a tragicomic show or play about human existence?
- The characters are almost never described physically: they reveal who they are through their actions or words. Taking this into account, are there certain ways each main character uses language which define them?
- In your opinion, why was the novel so successful?
- Compare the book with the film adaptation directed by Robert Mulligan. What differences can you find between the two versions?
- Can you see any parallel between America's segregated

society and Nazi Germany? If so, why?
- Explain the title of the book.

We want to hear from you!
Leave a comment on your online library
and share your favourite books on social media!

FURTHER READING

REFERENCE EDITION

- Lee, H. (1962) *To Kill a Mockingbird*. New York: Popular Library.

REFERENCE STUDIES

- Flynt, W. (2011) To Kill a Mockingbird. *Encyclopedia of Alabama*. [Online]. [Accessed 28 March 2017]. Available from: <http://www.encyclopediaofalabama.org/article/h-1140>
- Goodman, A. (2013) Rosa Parks at 100: a great American rebel for racial justice. *The Guardian*. [Online]. [Accessed 28 March 2017]. Available from: <https://www.theguardian.com/commentisfree/2013/jan/31/rosa-parks-100-american-rebel-justice>
- Hauser, S. (2012) The Dream, the Reality: Civil Rights in the '60s and Today. *Workforce*. [Online]. [Accessed 28 March 2017]. Available from: <http://www.workforce.com/2012/04/10/the-dream-the-reality-civil-rights-in-the-60s-and-today/>
- The New York Times. (2015) *Map of 73 Years of Lynchings*. [Online]. [Accessed 28 March 2017]. Available from: <http://www.nytimes.com/interactive/2015/02/10/us/map-of-73-years-of-lynching.html?_r=2 >
- Salter, D. (2013) Scottsboro Trials. *Encyclopedia of Alabama*. [Online]. [Accessed 28 March 2017]. Available from: <http://www.encyclopediaofalabama.org/article/h-1456>

- Urofsky, M.I. (2015) Jim Crow Law. *Encyclopaedia Britannica*. [Online]. [Accessed 28 March 2017]. Available from: <https://www.britannica.com/event/Jim-Crow-law>
- Younge, G. (2013) Martin Luther King: the story behind his 'I have a dream' speech. *The Guardian*. [Online]. [Accessed 28 March 2017]. Available from: <https://www.theguardian.com/world/2013/aug/09/martin-luther-king-dream-speech-history>
- Zinn, H. (2013) *A People's History of the United States: 1492-Present*. 3rd ed. Abingdon-on-Thames: Routledge.

ADAPTATION

- *To Kill a Mockingbird*. (1962) [film]. Robert Mulligan, dir. United States: Brentwood Productions; Pakula-Mulligan.

MORE FROM BRIGHTSUMMARIES.COM

- Reading guide – *Go Set a Watchman* by Harper Lee.

www.brightsummaries.com

Ebook EAN: 9782806295330

Paperback EAN: 9782806295347

Legal Deposit: D/2017/12603/159

This guide was produced with the collaboration of Alexandre Randal for the chapter 'Laws to ratify racism' and the section 'Go Set a Watchman'.

Cover: © Primento

Digital conception by Primento, the digital partner of publishers.

Printed in Great Britain
by Amazon